54 Spiritual Blessings
in Christ

54 Spiritual Blessings in Christ

As Found in the Book of Ephesians

Leona J. Atkinson

IN COLLABORATION WITH

REV. RICHARD L. RICE

Atkinson Publishing
Portland, Oregon

Published by Atkinson Publishing
leonaslines@gmail.com

SGLY Ministry
www.smilegodlovesyou.org

ISBN: 978–1463734206

Interior design by Sherry Green
 text set in 11 pt Adobe Jenson Pro

Clip Art from: http://www.wpclipart.com/

Dedication

I dedicate this book to God, my Abba Father, who in His kindness, grace, and mercy has given me the faith to believe and receive His wonderful gift of Salvation and with that, has also abundantly supplied me with every Spiritual Blessing in the heavenly places.

Thank You God for giving me all I will ever need to succeed!

I dedicate this book to Jesus Christ, my Savior and Lord. It is because of Him that I have been able to receive all these wonderful Spiritual Blessings, for these Fifty Four Spiritual Blessings are only given to those in Christ.

Thank You Jesus, for what you did to make this possible in my life.

I dedicate this book to the Holy Spirit, Who now lives within me. It is His work in me that brings about the manifestation of each of these Spiritual Blessings and I thank Him that He helps me to walk in these Blessings daily.

Contents

12 Deliverance
Set free from God's judgement/wrath
Ephesians 2:5, 8

13 Enlightenment
The understanding & appreciation of our hope & inheritance
Ephesians 1:18

14 Eternal Glorying
We become eternal praise for His endless & limitless grace & mercy
Ephesians 2:7 & 3:11

15 Faith
Reliance upon the merits of Christ
Ephesians 1:15

16 Favor
He shows graciousness—gives generous approval
Ephesians 2:7

17 Filled with Christ
We are complete in Christ
Ephesians 1:23 & 3:19

18 Forgiveness
We have pardon for our sins, shortcomings & trespasses
Ephesians 1:7

19 Freedom
From Sin, from the Past, from Failure, from the Law, to Rest
Ephesians 2:2,3,8,9,14,15

20 Glory of His Inheritance
He receives an inheritance in us
Ephesians 1:6,18

21 Grace
Showed us un-merited favor—mercy
Ephesians 1:6 & 2:7,8

22 Heritage
Our portion as children of God
Ephesians 1:11

23 Holy
We are consecrated & set apart for Him—made saints
Ephesians 1:4

24 Hope
His calling to godliness or to Heaven—took us from no hope to hope
Ephesians 1:18 & 2:12-13

25 Inheritance
We have all that Jesus has—we are Co-Heirs with Christ
Ephesians 1:11,13,14,18

26 Intimacy with God
We are God's own children through Jesus Christ
Ephesians 1:5

27 Knowledge of His Will
He reveals His plan & purpose for our lives
Ephesians 1:9

28 Love
We love the saints—Christian brotherhood; God loved us—His love for us
Ephesians 1:4,15 & 2:4 & 3:17,19

29 Mercy
Experience God's loving-kindness without measure
Ephesians 2:4 & 3:19

30 New Life
We were made alive in Christ—dead to sin & recreated for good works
Ephesians 2:1,5,10

31 Obedience
We are now children with hearts of obedience to His will & way
Ephesians 2:2

32 Peace
Christ is our peace—harmony with God & His family
Ephesians 2:14,15,17

33 Power
We have Christ's power & strength in us
Ephesians 1:19 & 3:20

34 Praise Givers
We bring praise to Him
Ephesians 1:6, 12, 14

35 Predestined
He destined us—planned in love for us
Ephesians 1:5 & 2:10

36 Purpose
He has a purpose for us—a plan for us
Ephesians 1:9 & 2:10 & 3:11

37 Raised Up
Not only resurrected in Jesus, but exalted in & with Him
Ephesians 2:6

38 Reconciled
Brought us near to God, made us Heirs & reconciled us with believing Israel
Ephesians 2:13,16,18

39 Redemption
Christ redeemed us, bought us back, purchased us, paid for our sins
Ephesians 1:7,14

40 Rest
God did the work of salvation so we could find rest in Him
Ephesians 2:8

41 Revelation
Insight of truth
Ephesians 1:9,17

42 Riches
He lavished all the riches of His grace upon us—the rich treasury of His glory
Ephesians 1:7,8 & 2:7 & 3:16

43 Salvation
We are saved from the power & penalty of sin
Ephesians 2:5,8

44 Sanctified
We are set apart & receive a purpose in life: serving Him by 'good works'
Ephesians 1:4 & 2:10

45 Sealed
His Spirit indwells us, a guarantee of our inheritance. He's our security deposit
Ephesians 1:13-14

46 Seated
God raised us up with Christ to sit with Him
Ephesians 2:6

47 Strength
Strengthened & reinforced with mighty power in the inner man
Ephesians 3:16

Blessed be the God and Father of our Lord Jesus Christ, who has blessed us with every spiritual blessing in the heavenly places in Christ...

Ephesians 1:3

Introduction

Perhaps you, like me, had read the verse Ephesians 1:3 many times and wondered just what those spiritual blessings were. If we had "every spiritual blessing," what were they and what did "in the heavenly places in Christ'" actually mean?

Well, recently I just got a wonderful answer to those questions which I wanted to share. My pastor had been doing weekly sermons on the book of Ephesians and when he first started the series I asked him about this verse and if he could tell me just what "every spiritual blessing" meant. He told me that I could find out by reading Ephesians chapters one through three, for in them Paul lists the spiritual blessings believers receive in Christ.

That set me off on an adventure and between what I found, and what my pastor added, I have recorded fifty-four spiritual blessings that believers have been given in Christ, just from chapters one through three in Ephesians! These blessings are all given at the moment of salvation. The moment a person accepts Christ he or she is not only blessed with salvation but with fifty-three other spiritual blessings as well.

My pastor explained it in an easy to understand way. One Sunday evening at church he made each of us a delicious banana split. As he assembled all the ingredients for this, he marked them individually—the bowl was marked "Christ", and each flavor of ice cream, the banana, all the flavorings, and the toppings were each marked with the name of a spiritual blessing.

The point was that Christ, being the bowl, held everything else, so when you accepted the bowl you got all the other good things in it!

That night was a revelation to many because as the pastor held out the bowl representing Christ with all the good things in it depicting many of the spiritual blessings, he offered it to us free, it didn't cost us anything, all we had to do was take it. He didn't ask us to do anything to earn it. He just offered it free to everyone. This was a picture of God offering us His Son, Jesus.

That night some people wanted it, took it and said "Thank you." Others ignored it. Some weren't sure if it was really meant for them and others had excuses of why they couldn't accept it. Some didn't feel they needed it, and others didn't think they were worthy of it. Some felt that they should do something to pay for it, because they couldn't accept the fact it was "free." Others said, "What's the catch?" because they figured there had to be something behind it all—the pastor must have some hidden agenda for doing this. And then, sadly, some said, "I don't want it right now, I will wait until later..."

It is my hope that this book will show you just what believers receive when they accept Christ and what un-believers miss out on when they choose not to believe and receive Him.

1

Our Riches in Christ—
Spiritual Blessing—

Believers have been given:

Abundance

Now to Him who is able to do exceedingly abundantly above all that we ask or think, according to the power that works in us... Ephesians 3:20

B elievers, God dwells within us!
He is waiting for us to start believing this, so we can begin seeing Him work in us, and through us, to abundantly accomplish His plans and purposes in our lives and in the lives of others we meet or interact with daily.

He is waiting for us to ask for things that we would not even begin to think about asking for or to do things that we might possibly think we would never be able to do. Why? Because, in it all, He will bring glory to His name through us. *"Exceeding abundantly beyond all that we ask or think"* are the very things God specializes in doing.

God has given us this wonderful Spiritual Blessing in Christ. Now all we have to do is claim it and live daily in the abundance we have received.

WALK IT OUT—Prayer:

Dear God, thank You for this wonderful Spiritual Blessing of Abundance. I so want to claim it in my life and use it daily for Your glory. Please help me to truly believe I have received this blessing and then show me how I might put it into practice every day of my life.

My Personal Thoughts:

Our Riches in Christ—
Spiritual Blessing—

Believers have been given:

Acceptance

…to the praise of the glory of His grace, by which He made us accepted in the Beloved. Ephesians 1:6

Believers in Christ, God has accepted us, just as we are, and made us His very own! He has received us, dearly welcomed us in love. We need not ever again feel left out or rejected. We need not feel we are "less than" or un-welcome, for in Christ God has honored us with blessings. Even if the world shuns us, we can look in the mirror and say, "God has accepted me in Christ."

What a wonderful Blessing! What shall we do with it?

WALK IT OUT—*Prayer:*

Dear God, thank You for accepting me, just as I am. It is hard sometimes to believe You could do that, so I ask that You help me to remember this whenever I am feeling un-worthy or un-welcome. Help me to focus on this truth when I am rejected by the world or left out socially, and give me the strength and wisdom I need to put this belief into action daily for Your praise and glory.

My Personal Thoughts:

Our Riches in Christ—
Spiritual Blessing—

Believers have been given:

Access

*For through Him we both have access by one Spirit to the Father...
Ephesians 2:18*

*...in whom we have boldness and access with confidence through faith in
Him. Ephesians 3:12*

In Christ, God has given us the right to come before Him in prayer. Believers, in Christ, we have been given the ability, and right or permission, to enter into God's presence, to approach His throne, to speak with Him—anytime, anywhere. As a believer in Christ, we have been given free admittance to God's throne room. We don't need to go to or through anyone else. Because of our faith in Christ, we can come boldly and with confidence to speak with God about anything.

We have been given this Blessing—now what will we do with it?

WALK IT OUT—*Prayer:*

Dear God, thank You so much for this privilege You have given me. It is an honor that I have been given access to come before You anytime, day or night, to speak with You about whatever is on my heart. Help me to not waste any time or opportunity in worrying or waiting or asking others to pray for me— but to always remember this free access is available to me, so that I quickly and confidently come before You with any cares or concerns I may have. And may I know that when I do, You will listen and respond to me.

My Personal Thoughts:

Our Riches in Christ—
Spiritual Blessing—

Believers have been:

Adopted

> *...having predestined us to adoption as sons by Jesus Christ to Himself, according to the good pleasure of His will... Ephesians 1:5*

Believers, God has made us His very own children! Why did He do this? *"According to the good pleasure of His will."* He wanted to receive us into a new relationship with Him, so that when we, by faith, had accepted Christ, God adopted us as His own.

To adopt means to legally take as one's own one who formerly was not. As believers in Christ, we now legally belong to God—we are His very own children. We are sons and daughters of the most High God.

What shall we do this Blessing?

WALK IT OUT—Prayer:

Father God, I am so thankful You chose to adopt me and make me Your own. I feel so glad to be Your child. As my Father, please help me daily to really know and believe what it means to be Your child and show me how I can live that out to bring glory to Your name. I want to be a good child who knows You, obeys You, and has a loving relationship with You daily.

My Personal Thoughts:

Our Riches in Christ—
Spiritual Blessing—

Believers have been given:

Blamelessness

...just as He chose us in Him before the foundation of the world, that we should be holy and without blame before Him in love... Ephesians 1:4

As believers in Christ we are without blame before God. Our sins are wiped away in Christ and God can look at us in love, without any blame, because we have accepted His Son, Jesus. In Christ we are declared "not guilty" of any sins—past, present, future. What freedom it is to know that we are blameless in God's sight and when He looks upon us He sees no fault, no blemish.

Having received such a Blessing as this, now what shall we do with it?

WALK IT OUT—Prayer:

Jesus, I thank You that in You I can be blameless in God's sight. Because of what You did at Calvary I can live and walk in freedom instead of in guilt and shame. I can stand before God who will look at me in love, because the faults and blemishes have been washed away by Your blood, Jesus. I cannot thank You enough for all You have done for me and I want to live my life daily just to please You for this wonderful Spiritual Blessing!

My Personal Thoughts:

Our Riches in Christ—
Spiritual Blessing—

Believers have been given:

Blessings

Blessed be the God and Father of our Lord Jesus Christ, who has blessed us with every spiritual blessing in the heavenly places in Christ... Ephesians 1:3

Believers, in Christ, God has given us every Spiritual Blessing! He did not hold anything back. He richly supplied us with all we will ever need or want. He has presented us with all the Spiritual Blessings in His heavenly storehouse. He has shown us His divine favor in providing all of this to us.

Now it is up to us to stop asking for more and to start using what we have already been given.

WALK IT OUT—Prayer:

Dear Heavenly Father, I am so grateful that You have blessed me with everything I will ever need spiritually. I want to learn just what that means so I can live it and share it with others. I want to remember daily that I am blessed and give You thanks for that. I want to start believing and living in those Blessings, instead of always asking You to give me what You have already provided to me. Help me Father, to learn and grow. I want to begin my day, every day, by saying, "I am Blessed!" and then to go out and bring glory to Your name by all I say and do.

My Personal Thoughts:

Our Riches in Christ—
Spiritual Blessing—

Believers are the:

Body of Christ

And He put all things under His feet, and gave Him to be head over all things to the church, which is His body, the fullness of Him who fills all in all. Ephesians 1:22-23

…having abolished in His flesh the enmity, that is, the law of commandments contained in ordinances, so as to create in Himself one new man from the two, thus making peace… Ephesians 2:15

Believers, we are the church—Christ's body on earth! God has made us Christ's body; Jesus is our Head, our Authority. We are filled with the fullness of Christ and in Christ we are all one.

We have been given this wonderful Spiritual Blessing to live out in our lives day to day.

WALK IT OUT—Prayer:

Dear God, this Blessing is most amazing to me! It is hard to imagine that I am the Body of Christ here on earth. However, since Your word tells me that this is so, I need to start believing it and living it out day by day. First of all I need to be sure I am thinking, saying and doing what the Head is telling me. If I am Christ's Body then my hands need to be doing His work, my feet need to be going where He would go and my speech needs to be His words. I also need to remember that every believer in Christ is His body and together we are all His church, therefore I need to be in unity with all true believers here on earth so we can accomplish the work He has for us to do. Dear God, thank You so much for this Blessing! Please help me to know how to live it out each day.

My Personal Thoughts:

Our Riches in Christ—
Spiritual Blessing—

Believers have been given:

Boldness

...in whom we have boldness and access with confidence through faith in Him. Ephesians 3:12

Believers, because of our faith in Christ, God has given us the Spiritual Blessing of Boldness, therefore we can be fearless and have courage to face anything that might rise up against us in this life. In Christ, we can come boldly before God's throne to ask Him for help in time of need. There is no reason to fear, or be hesitant.

We only need to remember who we are and what we have been blessed with and then go boldly forward to victory.

WALK IT OUT—*Prayer:*

Thank You God, for this Spiritual Blessing of Boldness. I am so glad that I no longer need to have any fear, but that I can be bold, and courageously come before You in my time of need. Thank You, that in Christ, this Boldness will result in victories in my life that will bring glory to Your name.

My Personal Thoughts:

Our Riches in Christ—
Spiritual Blessing—

Believers have been:

Chosen

...*just as He chose us in Him before the foundation of the world...*
Ephesians 1:4

Believers, God chose you to be His own even before you were born. He selected you before the foundation of the world. He picked you out before you were even thought about. Yes, before anyone on earth even pondered your birth or desired your presence, God chose you in Christ.

So, the next time someone rejects you or the enemy tries to push you aside, remind yourself that you are God's Chosen one, and you are a very special person to Him.

WALK IT OUT—Prayer:

I am a Chosen Child of God. I am important. I am special. I am wanted. I am valuable. My Father chose me before the foundation of this world. He wanted me to be His child before I was even thought of by anyone else. He loves me and wants me to remember that I have no need to feel rejected or un-wanted because I am Chosen to be His Child forever! Thank You Jesus for making this wonderful Blessing possible for me!

My Personal Thoughts:

Our Riches in Christ—
Spiritual Blessing—

Believers have been given:

Citizenship of Heaven

Now, therefore, you are no longer strangers and foreigners, but fellow citizens with the saints and members of the household of God… Ephesians 2:19

Because of our faith in Christ, we have been adopted as God's children and have become Citizens of Heaven. We are now entitled to become residents of the Household of God! We are now allowed all the privileges of Heaven. It is now our home and Christ is there now preparing a place for us to dwell with Him and our Father God someday. Because of our faith in Christ, we are no longer strangers or foreigners but we are fellow citizens with all the other saints who belong.

What a wonderful Blessing!

WALK IT OUT—*Prayer:*

Dear Father God, I am so blessed to be a part of Your family and to be a Citizen of Heaven. It is amazing to me that I am actually a member of Your household! Because of this, I want to remember who I am and keep my loyalties where they should be. Each day, I need to remind myself that this earthly life is just temporary, since someday I will be living forever in the place that Jesus is now preparing for me. Every day I want my focus to be on where my real home is. So, Father, as I dwell on this earth that sometimes wearies me, I pray that this knowledge can be something so wonderful for me to think upon and look forward to that I will always remember that I am now a Citizen of Heaven and a member of the Household of God! Thank You Father for this wonderful Blessing in Christ!

My Personal Thoughts:

11

Our Riches in Christ—
Spiritual Blessing—

Believers have been given:

Confidence

…in whom we have boldness and access with confidence through faith in Him. Ephesians 3:12

Through our faith in Christ we can have Confidence that we are blessed with every Spiritual Blessing. We can totally believe that we have all the Blessings we will ever need to live an abundant life here on earth and we can have full assurance that we will live an eternal life in Heaven with God our Father and Jesus, our Savior. We can put all our trust in this. We can fully rely on God's word. So let's live in complete Confidence every day, knowing we can depend on this truth.

Let's believe it, so we can walk in it, and in doing so, bless others with our Confidence.

WALK IT OUT—Prayer:

Dear God, I want to live in this Blessing every day. I want this Confidence to show in my life so as to let the world know that I am relying on You and Your word. Daily, as I move forward, walking in Your will, clothed in Confidence, I will be a living witness of Your grace and mercy. In this way, others will see how You have blessed me with Confidence and this might cause them to believe and receive these Blessings in Christ also. Thank You, Father God for this Blessing of Confidence.

My Personal Thoughts:

Our Riches in Christ—
Spiritual Blessing—

Believers have been given:

Deliverance

…even when we were dead in trespasses, (God) made us alive together with Christ (by grace you have been saved)… Ephesians 2:5

We were dead in our sins, doomed to destruction, yet God in His great mercy and grace delivered us and made us alive in Christ! Think about that! The moment we believed in Christ and accepted Him as our Lord and Savior, God set us free from the bonds of death. By God's grace, our belief in Christ delivered us from sin, which leads to death, and made us alive with Christ. We are no longer under God's wrath or judgment for we have received freedom in Christ!

What a wonderful Blessing Deliverance is!

Walk it out—Prayer:

Dear God, I am so thankful for the Deliverance You have given me in Christ. I, who was once dead in my sins, have been set free and made alive! I have been released from bondage and no longer need to fear Your judgment or wrath. What a wonderful Blessing! I am so happy to have received this! Now I need to go out and share this message of Deliverance with all those I meet. I need to seize every opportunity to share this news with others who might need to receive this Blessing also. I pray that I will be able to do that in some way, every day, God, as a thanksgiving to You for Your wonderful grace to me.

My Personal Thoughts:

13

Our Riches in Christ—
Spiritual Blessing—

Believers have been given:

Enlightenment

…the eyes of your understanding being enlightened; that you may know what is the hope of His calling, what are the riches of the glory of His inheritance in the saints… Ephesians 1:18

Believers, one of our Spiritual Blessings in Christ is that our eyes are no longer blinded by sin and our minds are no longer darkened. Through our belief in Jesus, God's light has been shed upon us, and His Holy Spirit has come to dwell within us to impart to us the ability to understand God's word intellectually and spiritually.

We have been blessed with this Enlightenment so that we can know, understand and appreciate our hope and inheritance in Christ.

WALK IT OUT—*Prayer:*

Thank You God for this Blessing of Enlightenment. I am so glad I am no longer "in the dark" spiritually. Now, I no longer need to be confused or puzzled by spiritual things or mystified by Your word because You have given me the ability to understand and grow in the knowledge of Your word and will. I can now be informed and edified as Your light illuminates my spiritual understanding. I am so grateful to have Your Holy Spirit dwelling within me, shedding light, revealing truth and instructing me daily.

My Personal Thoughts:

14

Our Riches in Christ—
Spiritual Blessing—

Believers have been given:

Eternal Glorying

...*that in the ages to come He might show the exceeding riches of His grace in His kindness toward us in Christ Jesus. Ephesians 2:7*

...*according to the eternal purpose which He accomplished in Christ Jesus our Lord... Ephesians 3:11*

Believers, we become eternal praise for His endless and limitless grace and mercy!

This means that throughout the endless ages to come you are going to be dwelling with God in His eternal kingdom as God is revealing unto you the exceeding richness of His mercy and kindness towards you through Christ Jesus. All the things that God has given and provided and done for you through Jesus Christ will be yours forever and you will never discover them all because eternity isn't long enough!

Isn't it amazing that this is His eternal purpose and we as believers are now a part of that!

WALK IT OUT—*Prayer:*

Wow! It is almost too much to comprehend that I would be a part of something of such magnitude! Thank You, God! Thank You, Jesus! I am so blessed by the knowledge that Your eternal purpose is that I will become eternal praise for Your endless and limitless grace and mercy. This is just too great to keep to myself! I must share it with others so they can rejoice with me and give You thanks for this wonderful Blessing!

My Personal Thoughts:

15

Our Riches in Christ—
Spiritual Blessing—

Believers have been given:

Faith

Therefore I also, after I heard of your faith in the Lord Jesus and your love for all the saints, Ephesians 1:15

For by grace you have been saved through faith; and that not of yourselves: it is the gift of God... Ephesians 2:8

In whom we have boldness and access with confidence through faith in Him. Ephesians 3:12

That Christ may dwell in your hearts by faith... Ephesians 3:17

Faith is reliance upon the merits of Christ. It is a complete confidence and trust in Jesus because of what He did for us. This Faith is a gift of God. It is part of the whole package of Blessings we receive when we accept Christ. We are beginning to see how blessed we are in Christ because even our Faith to believe is one of the Blessings!

How can this be? It is hard for our finite minds to comprehend that our salvation is of God alone, we have done nothing to achieve it, because even the Faith with which we believe has come from God!

How thankful we believers should be for this wonderful Blessing of Faith!

WALK IT OUT—*Prayer:*

Father God, it is hard for my finite mind to comprehend all that You have given me in Christ. Therefore, I am not going to try and figure it out but I am just going to accept it as a Blessing from You and thank you for the Faith You have blessed me with. Help me to walk in this Faith daily, and give me the ability to share the knowledge of it with others. May it make them aware that they should seek You and that, by so doing, they too will be able to receive this wonderful Blessing. For Paul said in Hebrews 11:6 *"without faith it is impossible to please Him (God), for he who comes to God must believe that He is, and that He is a rewarder of those who diligently seek Him."*

My Personal Thoughts:

16

Our Riches in Christ—
Spiritual Blessing—

Believers have been given:

Favor

...that in the ages to come He might show the exceeding riches of His grace in His kindness toward us in Christ Jesus. Ephesians 2:7

Favor is something done or granted out of goodwill rather than from justice, entitlement, effort, or for remuneration. It is a kind act. Isn't it a wonderful feeling to be favored! When you receive Favor you are given preference, you are treated with partiality, and it makes you feel liked, approved. Favor is one of the Spiritual Blessings we believers receive when we accept Christ. God shows us His Favor. He shows His graciousness to us. He gives us generous approval.

Think about that—isn't that a wonderful Blessing!

WALK IT OUT—Prayer:

Thank You Jesus, for giving me the opportunity to be favored by God. In thinking upon this I feel so special. I wish everyone could know the wonderful Blessings that are available to those who believe in You, Jesus. I hope each day that my life will reflect the Favor I receive from God, so others will see it and will want it in their lives also.

My Personal Thoughts:

Our Riches in Christ—
Spiritual Blessing—

Believers have been:

Filled With Christ

And He put all things under His feet, and gave Him to be head over all things to the church, which is His body, the fullness of Him who fills all in all. Ephesians 1: 22-23

to know the love of Christ which passes knowledge; that you may be filled with all the fullness of God. Ephesians 3:19

Believers, we are occupied to full capacity with Christ! God has made us full. The fullness of God as a Triune being in us is: 1, the fullness of God the Father (3:19); 2, the fullness of Jesus (4:13); and 3, the fullness of the Holy Spirit (5:18). How amazing is that! God put as much as can be held into us the moment we believed and accepted Jesus!

He plentifully supplied all we need to live our lives abundantly every day.

WALK IT OUT—*Prayer:*

Father God, it is so amazing to think that I am complete in Christ. There is nothing I need that is not already supplied to me. I am Filled with all the fullness of You and the more I give away to others, the more You pour into me. Thank You for filling me so completely that I will never need anything more. I give You all my thanks and praise for this wonderful Blessing!

My Personal Thoughts:

Our Riches in Christ—
Spiritual Blessing—

Believers have been given:

Forgiveness

In Him we have redemption through His blood, the forgiveness of sins, according to the riches of His grace... Ephesians 1:7

Believers, in Christ, we have pardon for our sins, shortcomings and trespasses. Our sin-debt, past, present and future, was paid for by Christ at the cross. In Him we have been forgiven and set free.

I am sure you know how good it feels to be forgiven by someone. At some time or another you have probably done or said something you were sorry for. When you said you were sorry and asked for Forgiveness, wasn't it wonderful to hear "Yes, I forgive you"? Those words set you free and brought new life.

That is what we have been given in Christ. The moment we believed and accepted Jesus, God said, "I forgive you, My child. You are now washed clean by the blood of My Son. Walk now in the freedom Jesus has provided for you."

WALK IT OUT—*Prayer:*

Oh what a Blessing Forgiveness is. Oh what a Blessing indeed.
To have my sins all washed away and from God's wrath to be freed.
Oh what Blessing Forgiveness is. Let me now never forget.
The wonderful freedom received in Christ as His blood washed away my debt.

Yes, what a wonderful Blessing Forgiveness is! To have my debt canceled, to be granted pardon, even when I was guilty, is more than I can even fathom. I want to sing about it and shout it out to the rooftops! Thank You so much Jesus for dying to set me free from sin and death. Thank You so much God for your grace and mercy. I pray I can share this wonderful Blessing with all I meet so everyone can know the freedom there is in Christ!

My Personal Thoughts:

Our Riches in Christ—
Spiritual Blessing—

Believers have been given:

Freedom

...in which you once walked according to the course of this world, according to the prince of the power of the air, the spirit who now works in the sons of disobedience, among whom also we all once conducted ourselves in the lusts of our flesh, fulfilling the desires of the flesh and of the mind, and were by nature children of wrath, just as the others. Ephesians 2:2-3

For by grace you have been saved through faith, and that not of yourselves; [it is] the gift of God, not of works, lest anyone should boast. Ephesians 2:8-9

For He Himself is our peace, who has made both one, and has broken down the middle wall of separation, having abolished in His flesh the enmity, [that is], the law of commandments [contained] in ordinances, so as to create in Himself one new man [from] the two, [thus] making peace... Ephesians 2:14-15

Believers, we have Freedom, Liberty, and Independence! In Christ we have been set free from sin, from the past, from failure, from the Law, and have been given the freedom to rest.

Before we accepted Christ we were being held captive by satan, we were bound by sin, disobedient children, under God's wrath, fulfilling the desires of the flesh and mind, separated from God and walking with the enemy, having no peace, knowing no joy.

But now, in Christ, we have been set free from the chains of sin and satan. We have become children of God, able to fulfill the plan and purpose He has for us. We can walk with Him, doing the good works He predestined for us to do and we can know His peace and His joy.

We are new creations in Christ! Hallelujah! We are free! Free to be who He created us to be!

WALK IT OUT—*Prayer:*

Dear Father God, this Freedom I have received is such a wonderful Blessing that words cannot express how I feel, so I will just give You all my thanks and praise every day and commit myself to walking with You daily, serving You by doing all the good works You have prepared for me to do. I thank You that I can enjoy peace and joy in my life now, even when my circumstances are not the best, and I can know I am Your child and rest in You whenever I am in need. Help me to know how to share the knowledge of this wonderful Blessing of Freedom with those I meet who might still be captives because I know You want everyone to be free and enjoy the wonders of Your mighty love.

My Personal Thoughts:

Our Riches in Christ—
Spiritual Blessing—

Believers are the:

Glory of His Inheritance

…the eyes of your understanding being enlightened; that you may know what is the hope of His calling, what are the riches of the glory of His inheritance in the saints… Ephesians 1:18

"There is a glory in this inheritance, riches of glory, rendering the Christian more excellent and more truly honorable than all about him:" [Matthew Henry]

Believers, in Christ, we have become God the Father's Inheritance! In Christ we not only receive an inheritance from God we also *become* His Inheritance!

At the resurrection, God the Father will receive His Glorious Inheritance (1:18), the saints, those who have been purchased through the glorious grace (1:6) of the glorious Father (1:17).

WALK IT OUT—Prayer:

Dear Father God, it is amazing that I not only have received a Glorious Inheritance *from* You, but that I also am a Glorious Inheritance *for* You. I am Your delight, a wonderful treasure in Your eyes. You see me as Your heritage, brilliantly beautiful, magnificent, the riches of Your glory in Christ. I have become Your Inheritance through Jesus. I hope I can grasp this awesome revelation and walk in its knowledge daily seeing myself as You see me.

My Personal Thoughts:

Our Riches in Christ—
Spiritual Blessing—

Believers have been given:

Grace

...in whom we have redemption through His blood, the forgiveness of sins, according to the riches of His grace... Ephesians 1:7

...even when we were dead in trespasses, [He] made us alive together with Christ (by grace you have been saved)... Ephesians 2:5

For by grace you have been saved through faith, and that not of yourselves; it is the gift of God... Ephesians 2:8

What is GRACE? The Dictionary[1] defines it as: favor or good will, mercy; clemency; pardon: the freely given, unmerited favor and love of God.

So, believers, it is because of the unmerited favor of God that we are saved. It is by His favor or goodwill that we have forgiveness of sins. It is because of His mercy that we have been redeemed. We have received the gift of salvation because of God's pardon.

What a wonderful blessing God's Grace is!

WALK IT OUT—*Prayer:*

Dear God, I am so thankful for Your Grace. If not for this blessing I would not have the wonderful gifts of faith and salvation, for there is no way I could have received those on my own. I want to always remember that if not for Your Grace, I would still be a helpless sinner, lost and in darkness with no hope. I want to give You thanks every day for this wonderful Blessing of Grace by letting others know about it. Help me to know how to share the truth of this wonderful blessing with all those I meet.

1 Paraphrased from Dictionary.com, "grace," in Collins English Dictionary - Complete & Unabridged 10th Edition

My Personal Thoughts:

Our Riches in Christ—
Spiritual Blessing—

Believers have been given:

Heritage

In Him (Christ) we also were made [God's] heritage (portion)...
Ephesians 1:11 [Amplified Bible]

Heritage is a birthright. It is something that comes to you by birth. When we believed and received Christ, we received an inheritance from God—we became co-heirs with Christ. However, at that time we also became God's Heritage, for because of our rebirth, we became His possession, His glory.

On earth we might be born into a family of wealth, power or prestige. This would be our earthly Heritage, our birthright. Spiritually, when we are born again, we are born into God's family, we become His Heritage, His portion: *"...for the LORD's portion is His people..."* [Deuteronomy 32:9].

Think about this: if all true believers are God's Heritage we must be very careful how we treat one another for God looks upon each believer as His glory [Eph 1:12], His jewels [Mal.3:17], His treasures [2 Cor.4:7], and His very own possessions [Eph.1:14]. Why? Because believers reflect Him to the world. They are filled with Him. Each one is His Heritage and brings glory to His name. Believers are *"the riches of His glory"* in Christ (Ephesians 3:16).

WALK IT OUT—Prayer:

Dear God, it is hard for me to imagine how I can be Your Heritage, but Your word tells me that I am. I see that just by my sharing with others I am a believer, this gives You glory because it is a testimony to Your grace and mercy. When I realize that You even gave me the faith to believe, it is to Your glory also—for it shows Your great love and kindness. When I shine the light that You put within me, others see You and this brings You glory. I am Your Heritage, a jar of clay, molded by You, my Potter (Isaiah 64:8). I am filled with You, and as You are poured out through me each day, others are able to see Your great power and this brings glory to You. I am so glad to be Your Heritage and I want to join together with all believers to bring more praise and glory to Your name!

My Personal Thoughts:

Our Riches in Christ—
Spiritual Blessing—

Believers have been given:

Holiness

just as He chose us in Him before the foundation of the world, that we should be holy and without blame before Him in love... Ephesians 1:4

Believers, because of our faith in Christ we are Holy! God has blessed us with Holiness! Now, to be Holy does not mean to be perfect or sinless. HOLY means something that is set aside for a special purpose. So, this Spiritual Blessing of Holiness means that God has chosen us and set us aside for a special purpose He had planned for us before the foundation of the world!

God, because of His great love for us, chose us in Christ and blessed us to be consecrated and set apart for Him. He blessed us with His Holiness when we accepted Christ, so we could become His saints, dedicated to serve Him and devoted to achieving the plan and purpose He has for each of us.

WALK IT OUT—*Prayer:*

Dear Father God, thank You for this Blessing of Holiness, for with it I can be separated from the world and sanctified for You. I want to be dedicated to Your service, God—set apart from the world and self. This Blessing allows me to be a saint who is devoted to You and active in Your service daily. I pray that as I walk in Your blessings others will be able to see them in me and be drawn to You because of it.

My Personal Thoughts:

Our Riches in Christ—
Spiritual Blessing—

Believers have been given:

Hope

...the eyes of your understanding being enlightened; that you may know what is the hope of His calling... Ephesians 1:18

...that at that time you were without Christ, being aliens from the commonwealth of Israel and strangers from the covenants of promise, having no hope and without God in the world. But now in Christ Jesus you who once were far off have been brought near by the blood of Christ. Ephesians 2:12-13

As believers we are blessed with Hope! Hope is a feeling that what is wanted will happen. It is a desire accompanied by expectation. It is a promise, a declaration that something will or will not be done.

Our belief in Christ has taken us from the condition of "no hope" to HOPE! As believers, we are no longer without God in this world. We are no longer far off from Him but have now been brought near by the blood of Christ. He has given us the Hope of heaven. He has given us the Hope of godliness. Each day we can live in the expectation that what He has promised will be given to us.

Thank God for the Hope that is now in us!

WALK IT OUT—*Prayer:*

Dear Father God, I am so thankful for this Blessing of Hope! Because of it I can look forward to spending eternity with You! But, also, because of Hope, I can look forward to living a life here on earth that is pleasing to You. I can expect that the life of godliness which You have called me to is possible for me to live. I can know that the feeling that what is wanted can be had, or that events in my life will turn out for the best, even though they may not seem so at the time. Because of Hope I can trust, expect and rest assured that You are in control of all things and that I have a place in Your plans. Thank You, Father God, for Hope. It is my very life breath each day!

My Personal Thoughts:

Our Riches in Christ—
Spiritual Blessing—

Believers have been given:

Inheritance

...in Him also we have obtained an inheritance... Ephesians 1:11

Inheritance can be property or possessions given to an heir by the owner. An heir is a person who inherits or has a right of inheritance of the property of another.

When we believed and received Jesus we became children of God and co-heirs with Christ. Therefore, everything the Father gave to Jesus—we now have also because we are co-heirs. Isn't it amazing to realize that we have all that Jesus has!

"All of God's riches in heaven and earth are all rolled up into the Savior! And we will inherit all those good things simply because we trusted in Christ!!"[2]

Believers, we are rich! Everyday we should remember and give thanks for our inheritance in Christ! We should live daily as Children of God who are Co-Heirs with Christ to all the blessings and riches of God!

WALK IT OUT—*Prayer:*

Dear Father God, I am so glad for this inheritance You've given me in Christ! Just the thought of being a co-heir with Jesus is amazing! Then to think that I have received all of Your riches in heaven and earth, it is mind-boggling! How do I begin to walk this out daily? How do I begin to live in this inheritance I have received? Day by day, I need to remind myself of who I am and what I have received so that I can use this inheritance on earth for Your glory. I need to make the most of each day so I can be a wise steward of all these wonderful riches You have blessed me with! Then I need to share the knowledge of this with others so they too can know, believe and receive.

2*John Brown's Commentary on Ephesians 1*, Brown, John. "Ephesians 1." *Blue Letter Bible*. 15 Jul 2003. 2011. 25 Jul 2011.<blueletterbible.org>

My Personal Thoughts:

Our Riches in Christ—
Spiritual Blessing—

Believers have been given:

Intimacy With God

having predestined us to adoption as sons by Jesus Christ to Himself, according to the good pleasure of His will, Ephesians 1:5

…Once you were far away from God, but now you have been brought near to Him through the blood of Christ. Ephesians 2:13 (New Living Translation)

Believers, because of our faith in Jesus Christ we are now Sons and Daughters of the Most High God. We can legally call God our Father and not only that, we can call Him our Abba Father, our Papa! We can now have a close, personal relationship with God our Father. As His children we have Intimacy with Him.

This Blessing is something to be treasured and one we should be thankful for every minute of every day!

WALK IT OUT—*Prayer:*

Dear Father God, my Abba Father, I thank You for adopting me and making me your child. I thank You that I am now blessed to have a close, personal relationship with You, the Most High God of the Universe! That is a special Blessing and one that I want to remember every day of my life. I want to remind myself every day that I, who once was a child of wrath, am now a Child of Blessing, not because of anything I did, but only because of the good pleasure of Your will. Thank you Father for that, and as I live in this world, one of my daily goals will be to tell everyone I meet about the Great and Wonderful Father that I have.

My Personal Thoughts:

Our Riches in Christ—
Spiritual Blessing—

Believers have been given:

Knowledge of His Will

having made known to us the mystery of His will, according to His good pleasure, which He purposed in Himself, Ephesians 1:9

God's secret plan has now been revealed to us; it is a plan centered on Christ, designed long ago according to God's good pleasure. Ephesians 1:9 (New Living Translation)

One of the Spiritual Blessings that we Believers in Christ receive, is that God reveals His plan and purpose for our lives. God always had a plan for us. He created us for a purpose. His greatest plan and purpose is that we would come to know Him. However, before we believed and received Christ we were blinded to His wonderful plan—it was a secret to us. But, now, as Believers, God's will has been revealed to us through the pages of the Bible and we can walk in His will daily. He makes His will plain to His children (believers), including that we *"Rejoice always, pray without ceasing, in everything give thanks; for this is the will of God in Christ Jesus for you."* (1 Thessalonians 5:16-18).

This Blessing we receive in Christ, is that God's truth is fully disclosed to us, giving us everything necessary for Knowing God and living for Him. What great riches we receive in Christ!!

WALK IT OUT—*Prayer:*

I thank You Father, for making it possible for me to have the Knowledge of Your Will. I thank You that, in Christ, I am no longer blinded to Your ways. I thank You that my mind is no longer darkened to Your truth. Thank You, that Your Will for my life is no longer a secret, but it is a plan and purpose for good that You are making known to me daily. I pray each day that I can see and know more and more of Your Will, so I can fulfill the plan and purpose You have created me for.

My Personal Thoughts:

Our Riches in Christ—
Spiritual Blessing—

Believers have been given:

Love

Long ago, even before He made the world, God loved us and chose us in Christ to be holy and without fault in his eyes...and He loved us so very much, that even while we were dead because of our sins, He gave us life when He raised Christ from the dead. Ephesians 1:4, 2:4 (New Living Translation)

The song "Because of Your Love" (Paul Baloche) says:
*"Because of Your love, we're forgiven,
Because of Your love, our hearts are clean."*
God loved us! (When we were yet sinners).
God loved us so very much! (He sent His Son to die for us, while we were yet sinners).

It is something we should think about and remember every day! He gave us life, while we were dead! All those days before we knew Christ, when we were dead in our trespasses, blinded to the truth, living our lives for the world and ourselves—God loved us! What a wonderful Love that is! It is amazing!

And now, as Believers, that incredible Love is ours! The Love of God, the Love of Christ, is in us and because of that we can share it with others. Because this wonderful Love is one of the Spiritual Blessings we receive in Christ, we are able to love our brothers and sisters in Christ with the same Love that God has shown to us. This amazing un-conditional Love in us also makes it possible for us to love even our enemies. What an incredible un-ending gift Love is!

WALK IT OUT—Prayer:

Dear Father God, thank You for Your un-conditional Love for me. Thank You, Jesus for Your sacrificial Love for me. I am so grateful that I now have Your Love inside of me so that I am able to love others, not only my brothers and sisters in Christ, but also the lost who are in the world, those who You Love that need to come to know You and Your Son Jesus. I pray that I can put this Love You have given me into action each day of my life, so others will see the wonders of Your mighty Love through me and whatever their needs are they will be met because of Your Love.

My Personal Thoughts:

Our Riches in Christ—
Spiritual Blessing—

Believers have been given:

Mercy

> *But God, who is rich in mercy, because of His great love with which He loved us, Ephesians 2:4*

Rich in Mercy! Great in Love! What amazing adjectives are used to describe what we have been given!

It was because of His rich Mercy that we, who were lost in sin, were able to receive His gift of Salvation and now, as Believers, because of God's rich Mercy, we can experience His loving kindness without measure! There is no end to it—we can never come to the point where His Mercy and love towards us runs out!

Our God is full of compassion and He wants to bless us daily with His favor and love. He is ever merciful towards us, always willing to show us His pardon because we are in Christ.

WALK IT OUT—Prayer:

Dear Father God, I will try to remember this verse whenever I feel I don't measure up or when I have done something wrong. I will remind myself that in Christ, I have been blessed with Your gift of Mercy and so I have no need to worry, for as I confess my sins or shortcomings to You, I can be assured that You, my God, who is rich in Mercy and has a great love for me, will be ready and willing to forgive me and to show me Your great love. Thank You Father God, for this wonderful blessing of Mercy! I will treasure it daily and do my best to show Mercy to others as You have shown it to me.

My Personal Thoughts:

Our Riches in Christ—
Spiritual Blessing—

Believers have been given:

New Life

And you He made alive, who were dead in trespasses and sins,
Ephesians 2:1

This Spiritual Blessing is the gift of New Life! By believing and receiving
Jesus, we who were spiritually dead are made spiritually alive. Verses five
and six say, *"even when we were dead in trespasses, [God] made us alive together
with Christ (by grace you have been saved) and raised us up together, and made us
sit together in the heavenly places in Christ Jesus."*

When we believed and received Christ, we were "born again" and because of
this New Life, we now have the ability, in Christ, to live according to the plan
God has just for us.

WALK IT OUT—*Prayer:*

Dear God, what can I say except, "Thank You" for this New Life You have
given me! I know I was once spiritually dead, lost in sin, without hope and
now, because of Christ, I am a new person! I am alive spiritually, no longer
lost and without hope. I have been "born again" to a New Life with You!
How amazing is that! To think that I now have the ability in Christ, to live
out the plan and purpose You have just for me, one that is good and will
bring glory to Your name! It is so exciting to think about it that I can hardly
wait to experience it each day! Thank You! Thank You! I look forward to
each day of this New Life with You.

My Personal Thoughts:

Our Riches in Christ—
Spiritual Blessing—

Believers have been given:

Obedience

> You used to live in sin, just like the rest of the world, obeying the devil—
> the commander of the powers in the unseen world.³ He is the spirit at
> work in the hearts of those who refuse to obey God. Ephesians 2:2 (New
> Living Translation)

Believers, we no longer have to live like the rest of the world. Because of
Christ, we are no longer full of sin. We are now Children of God, with
hearts of Obedience to His will and way.

We have the Holy Spirit within us, working in our hearts and He gives us
the ability and desire to be Obedient to God.

WALK IT OUT—Prayer:

Dear God, I am so glad to be Your child and I realize that I am so blessed
that You have given me not only the ability to be obedient to Your way and
Will, but also the inclination to do so. I pray that Your Holy Spirit, who is now
living within me, will continue His work in my heart so that I will be able live
out my desire to totally submit to Your authority in all my life situations so
that I am seen by You as an obedient child with whom You are well pleased.

---

3 Greek: obeying the commander of the power of the air.

My Personal Thoughts:

Our Riches in Christ—
Spiritual Blessing—

Believers have been given:

$$\mathscr{P}\text{eace}$$

For He Himself is our peace, who has made both one, and has broken down the middle wall of separation, Ephesians 2:14

At Jesus' birth the angels announced that Peace and goodwill had come to earth for all men—*"Glory to God in the highest, and on earth peace, goodwill toward men!"* (Luke 2:14). That Peace and goodwill was Jesus Himself! Christ is our Peace. Because of Jesus all believers, whether Jew or Gentile, now have harmony with God and His family.

All of us are now one in Christ, there is no difference-—male, female, Jew, Gentile—we are all Children of God and His church.

WALK IT OUT—*Prayer:*

Dear Father God, my prayer is that I will focus on walking in the Peace of Christ each day. I pray that I will live out this Spiritual Blessing of Peace as I interact with other Believers I meet on a daily basis. I want to be an active part in the Family of God here on earth by getting to know as many of His Children as I can and fellowshipping with them. I pray that we Believers in Christ will be one big happy family that rejoices daily in what we have been given and so give glory to God our Father as we do. Thank You, Jesus, for coming to earth to be our Peace and so bringing us all together as one!

My Personal Thoughts:

Our Riches in Christ—
Spiritual Blessing—

Believers have been given:

Power

...and what is the exceeding greatness of His power toward us who believe, according to the working of His mighty power which He worked in Christ when He raised Him from the dead and seated Him at His right hand in the heavenly places, Ephesians 1:19,20

Now to Him who is able to do exceedingly abundantly above all that we ask or think, according to the power that works in us, Ephesians 3:20

Believers: we have Christ's Power and strength in us! His Power is at work in us daily! It is great—it is mighty. It is the same Power that raised Christ from the dead! It is an overcoming Power! This Power gives us victory over the world, ourselves and satan.

It enables us to do exceedingly and abundantly above all that we might ask or think to do!

WALK IT OUT—*Prayer:*

Dear God, I am so glad to know that I am blessed with the Power and strength of Jesus! It is amazing to realize that the Power of Jesus enables me to live in victory every day! No matter what my circumstances are, I need only to remember that nothing in my life is greater than the Power of Christ that is within me. I pray that I can keep this focus each day and so live a life that reflects His mighty Power, which is always working in an exceedingly abundant way in me. And I pray that this mighty Power, at work in me, will not only bring greatness to me but to all those whose lives I might touch, and so bring praise and glory to God.

My Personal Thoughts:

Our Riches in Christ—
Spiritual Blessing—

Believers have been made:

Praise-Givers

to the praise of the glory of His grace, by which He made us accepted in the Beloved. Ephesians 1:6

that we who first trusted in Christ should be to the praise of His glory. Ephesians 1:12

who is the guarantee of our inheritance until the redemption of the purchased possession, to the praise of His glory. Ephesians 1:14

By grace we are saved: "to the praise of His glory."

We are accepted in the Beloved: "to the praise of His glory."
Our faith and trust in Christ is: "to the praise of His glory."
The Holy Spirit dwelling in us as guarantee of our inheritance: "to the praise of His glory."
—Everything is to bring God praise! Just the fact that we are Believers brings Him praise!
Through all these things and more, we believers, give God praise.

Isn't it wonderful to think that we became Praise-Givers to God the moment we believed and received His Son Jesus! That thought alone should cause us to shout praises to Him with our mouths every day!

WALK IT OUT—*Prayer:*

Dear Father God, I am so glad to know that I am a Praise-Giver to You. It is amazing that my life is to be the praise of Your glory! I am so thankful that I believed and received Jesus as my Savior and Lord. Thank You for giving me the faith and grace to do that. It is my great desire to live out each day of my life here on earth as a Praise-Giver to You!

My Personal Thoughts:

Our Riches in Christ—
Spiritual Blessing—

Believers have been:

Predestined

having predestined us to adoption as sons by Jesus Christ to Himself, according to the good pleasure of His will... Ephesians 1:5

For we are His workmanship, created in Christ Jesus for good works, which God prepared beforehand that we should walk in them. Ephesians 2:10

Believers, we, (those who have accepted Christ as Savior), have been "chosen", "predestined", and "accepted"!! Predestined means "decided beforehand." Think of predestination like this: God the Father has Predestined (destined beforehand) us to be His children by adoption. Before time even began, He determined to make us His own children, though Jesus, for the express purpose of making us like Jesus (Romans 8:28-29).

That is what Paul is describing in Philippians 1:6, *"being confident of this very thing, that He who has begun a good work in you will complete it until the day of Jesus Christ."* Believers, this work of salvation has not only been begun in us, but God will finish and perfect it in us!

Human parents can bestow all kinds of blessings upon their adopted children: love, wealth, education, ethics and morality, but—the one thing they can't give is their own nature and character. Through predestination, however, God has chosen to make us in the image of His own Son, giving us not only all the riches and blessings available in Jesus, but also His very own Divine nature.

WALK IT OUT—Prayer:

Dear God, I am so glad that You Predestined me to be your child. It's such a big word and it is hard to understand, but I see from Your word, the Bible, that even before I came to believe, You had Predestined me to become Your child and prepared good works for me to do! It is so amazing to think that even before the world began, You thought of me and Predestined me to be Your own. You had a plan and purpose that only I could fulfill. You appointed me to be Your own and fulfill the good works You had planned for me to do, and then You created me, and I was Your workmanship. Amazing! Thank You God for who You are and what You do! You are so good and wonderful and I am so glad to be Your child!

My Personal Thoughts:

Our Riches in Christ—
Spiritual Blessing—

Believers have been given:

Purpose

In Him [Jesus] we were also chosen, having been predestined according to the plan of Him [God the Father] who works out everything in conformity with the purpose of His [God's] will... Ephesians 1:11 (New International Version)

According to the eternal purpose which he accomplished in Christ Jesus our Lord... Ephesians 3:11

Believers, God has a Purpose for us. He had a plan for us when He created us! Before we were even born, God had a Purpose for our lives! And it wasn't just any Purpose—it was a plan for good, a plan to give us a future and a hope! (Jere.29:11) Now...isn't that amazing! God makes His plan carefully according to an eternal Purpose, taking counsel within the Godhead, and then He works with all wisdom to accomplish it in our lives.

He *"works in you to will and to act according to his good purpose."* (Philippians 2:13 NIV) Isn't it exciting to realize that God has a specific Purpose for each of us, and that each day He is at work in us and around us to bring that Purpose into being?

WALK IT OUT—*Prayer:*

Dear God, this knowledge of You and Your plan and Purpose for me, is sometimes so hard for me to grasp. When I think of You, Your love, and all that You have done—all that You are doing, and will do for me and through my life—it just causes me to give You thanks for every minute of my life, knowing that You are working all things out for good according to Your Purpose and for Your glory. I am so glad that my life will somehow reflect the Purpose You have chosen and I look forward each day to walking according to the plan You are carefully working out for me. I will trust and believe that You are at work daily in my life, arranging and planning each circumstance and event, so that it will all bring glory to You and good to me! Thank You, God for my life and for all the Blessings in it!

My Personal Thoughts:

Our Riches in Christ—
Spiritual Blessing—

Believers have been:

Raised Up

...and raised us up together and made us sit together in the heavenly places in Christ Jesus. Ephesians 2:6

Believers, God not only resurrected us in Jesus, but He exalted us in Him and with Him. After Jesus' resurrection, He sat down on the right side of the Father in heaven. *His work was done* (Hebrews 1:3 and 10:12). His death on the cross was a completion of the Father's plan. When we believed and received Jesus, God also Raised us Up to a new life and seated us spiritually in the heavenly places with Christ signifying that our salvation was complete. Now there is nothing more to be done for us spiritually, with our salvation we have been blessed with many Spiritual Blessings and we are one with Christ, seated in the heavenly places with Him, a child of God and citizen of Heaven.

God has given us all the Spiritual Blessings we will ever need and even though we are still physically living here on earth, spiritually we have been exalted in and with Christ.

WALK IT OUT—Prayer:

Dear Father God, as I think about this word, I am physically here on earth, but I see that spiritually I am seated in the heavenly places with Christ. Therefore, I need to keep my eyes on things above and not on things on the earth. I need to remember to stay spiritually minded and not earthly minded. My focus needs to be on the heavenly places and my eternal home instead of this worldly place that I am physically living in, for it is not really my home. Help me Father to remember that You have blessed me with all these wonderful Spiritual Blessings that give me the ability to live spiritually minded here on earth, so I can keep my focus on enjoying my days sitting together with Jesus in the heavenly places!

My Personal Thoughts:

Our Riches in Christ—
Spiritual Blessing—

Believers have been:

Reconciled

But now in Christ Jesus you who once were far off have been brought near by the blood of Christ. Ephesians 2:13

and that He might reconcile them both to God in one body through the cross, thereby putting to death the enmity. Ephesians 2:16

RECONCILED means "made right." Christ's blood has brought Believers into peace and harmony with God. When Jesus shed His blood on the cross He made things right between us and God. He re-established a close relationship between God and man. He settled or resolved the hostility between Jews and Gentiles by making them both one in Christ.

So now those who were once far off from God, are near to Him, co-heirs with Christ and are one body—the Church, His Bride.

WALK IT OUT—*Prayer:*

Dear Father God, what a Blessing it is to know that I am Reconciled or made right with You! It is a Blessing to know that there is no longer a separation between me and You, but now, because of Christ's blood, I am one with You, and with believing Israel, in Christ. I hope to give thanks each day for this wonderful Blessing of Reconciliation, as I walk the Spirit, receiving all the benefits of being a co-heir with Christ, Reconciled to You, Father, by Your Son and enjoying the fellowship of my brothers and sisters in Christ. Thank you Jesus for making this wonderful Blessing available to me!

My Personal Thoughts:

Our Riches in Christ—
Spiritual Blessing—

Believers have been given:

Redemption

in Him we have redemption through His blood, the forgiveness of sins, according to the riches of His grace
Ephesians 1:7

Believers, if we stop to really realize what this verse is saying, we will be so overcome with gratitude for this Blessing we have received! The price Christ paid for our Redemption was costly beyond measure; it was His very lifeblood that He poured out for us. Stop and think about that!

He gave His all for us so we could be redeemed from sin and forgiven now and forever and someday we will receive our total Redemption when we leave our mortal bodies and enter heaven to live eternally with Christ, our Savior.

WALK IT OUT—Prayer:

Dear Father God, I am so grateful when I think about what I have received in Christ. Because of His death, I am set free from sin and it's captivity. I no longer need to live in bondage to sin, because Christ's blood has set me free. When I really stop to think about how wonderful this Blessing is I am overwhelmed with gratitude and I just want to give You all my thanks and praise for Your grace which made this all possible.

My Personal Thoughts:

40

Our Riches in Christ— Spiritual Blessing—

Believers have been given:

Rest

For by grace you have been saved through faith, and that not of yourselves; it is the gift of God, not of works, lest anyone should boast. Ephesians 2: 8-9

Yes, Believers, one of our Spiritual Blessings in Christ is REST! Doesn't that sound great! REST! It is something that is so needed; yet something that often eludes us in this busy world of striving and stress. REST is probably not something we think God blessed us with, but this verse in Ephesians tells us that God did all the work of salvation so we could find Rest in Him. It tells us that He provided the grace and even the faith with which we believed and received! We can take no credit for any of it. We did no work and we still do not need to do any work. All the work is done and we can enjoy resting in Him daily! He did the work so we could be set free—to rest in Him. That is really what He wants, don't you see? He wants us to just sit and rest with Him, to linger, to learn from Him and just enjoy being in His presence.

Jesus said: *"Come to Me, all you who labor and are heavy laden, and I will give you rest. Take My yoke upon you and learn from Me, for I am gentle and lowly in heart, and you will find rest for your souls. For My yoke is easy and My burden is light."* (Matthew 11:28-30)

WALK IT OUT—*Prayer:*

Dear Father God, I really hadn't thought much about this Spiritual Blessing of Rest before. But now that I see the truth of it, I am so comforted in the realization that I can just find Rest in You, for the work of Salvation is done, it is complete, and there is not one thing that needs yet to be done. Therefore, I can just be still and Rest in this thought daily. No need for me to feel burdened or to think I am somehow responsible for taking some action to earn Your favor. For the work is all done, and my job now is just to sit and Rest in You, listening to You, leaning on You and learning from You. This Blessing of Rest is so needed in this busy hectic world where we seem to always need to be striving and working to meet our needs or get ahead. Thank You, Father for the peace and tranquility of Rest! I hope to consider this Blessing more and more each day until I truly learn to completely Rest in You!

Cease from your action, your worry, your care.
Be settled, secure, for your burden I'll bear.
Enjoy My Blessings, one by one,
for the work of salvation has already been done.
So enter My Rest and lean on Me,
because My grace and mercy have set you free!

My Personal Thoughts:

_____

_____

_____

_____

_____

_____

_____

_____

_____

_____

_____

_____

_____

_____

_____

_____

_____

_____

_____

_____

41

Our Riches in Christ—
Spiritual Blessing—

Believers have been given:

Revelation

having made known to us the mystery of His will, according to His good pleasure which He purposed in Himself, Ephesians 1:9

that the God of our Lord Jesus Christ, the Father of glory, may give to you the spirit of wisdom and revelation in the knowledge of Him, Ephesians 1:17

In these verses we see God's disclosure of Himself, and His Will, to us Believers. Revelation is insight or unveiling of truth. When we believed and received Christ, God then blessed us with Revelation of Himself for the purpose of knowing Him better. He unveiled the mystery of Himself and His Will to us, so that His plan and purpose might no longer be hidden from us.

As Believers, we have been blessed with the ability to understand and know Him, His Will, and His divine truths in His word.

WALK IT OUT—*Prayer:*

God, I am so thankful for this Spiritual Blessing of Revelation. It is wonderful to know that in Christ, I have been given insight of truth, and that this truth is no longer a mystery, but it is unveiled, out in the open for me to understand and know because of this Blessing in Christ! Jesus said the Holy Spirit would guide us into all truth (John 16:13). Thank You, Father for sending Him to do so for me, and thank You for Your Word, which is truth. Thank You for Blessing me with Revelation and Wisdom to understand Your word, and for Knowledge, so I can know You better and become fully acquainted with You!

My Personal Thoughts:

Our Riches in Christ—
Spiritual Blessing—

Believers have been given:

Riches

In Him we have redemption through His blood, the forgiveness of sins, according to the riches of His grace, which He made to abound toward us in all wisdom and prudence... Ephesians 1:7-8

that in the ages to come He might show the exceeding riches of His grace in His kindness toward us in Christ Jesus. Ephesians 2:7

that He would grant you, according to the riches of His glory, to be strengthened with might through His Spirit in the inner man... Ephesians 3:16

Believers, God has lavished all the Riches of His grace upon us! "Riches of His Grace" could be called "Abundance of His Favor" or "Great Wealth of His Mercy" or "Treasures of His Goodwill" for He has generously given us every Spiritual Blessing to use now, in the present day, and these Blessings are continuous because His Riches know no bounds! There is not a day when we Believers are not Blessed! There is not a day when we will ever use up all God's Riches, for He has an endless supply and they are all given for us to use for His glory! Just look at the above three scripture verses and you will see just a few of the Riches God has blessed us with: Redemption, Forgiveness, Wisdom, Kindness, Strength, Power, and Holy Spirit.

What wonderful treasures we have been given in Christ!

WALK IT OUT—*Prayer:*

Dear God, I am so rich in Christ! For, in Your grace, You have showered me with Your Riches of Blessings upon Blessings! I should never say I am poor and needy, for in Christ I have a treasure greater than anything I could ever imagine! The Riches You have so abundantly bestowed upon me will never run out for they are an endless supply of wealth that I will never be able to exhaust, no matter how much I use them. Thank You, Father God, for these wonderful Riches! Because of Your grace I can live each day bountifully blessed with all I will ever need or want to live this life according to Your plan and purpose for me and I pray that I may wisely use all these Riches to bring glory and honor to Your name.

My Personal Thoughts:

Our Riches in Christ—
Spiritual Blessing—

Believers have been given:

Salvation

even when we were dead in trespasses, [God] made us alive together with Christ (by grace you have been saved)... Ephesians 2:5

For by grace you have been saved through faith, and that not of yourselves; it is the gift of God... Ephesians 2:8

Believers, when we received Salvation, by the grace of God we were saved from the power and penalty of sin. Salvation delivered us from sin once and for all. Before Salvation we were in bondage to sin and receiving it's wages of death. Now, however, sin's power over us is gone, and its debt of death has been paid by Christ, so this blessing of Salvation gives us freedom from sin and a brand new life!

Now, receiving those Blessings from Salvation is most wonderful in itself, but that is not all we have received from Salvation, there is so much more that is included! Think of it this way: imagine Salvation as a big beautiful gift box that is being handed to you by God. When you accept it and open it you find that inside that gift of Salvation is much more than you could have ever imagined, for inside Salvation you will find all the other Spiritual Blessings in Christ!

WALK IT OUT—*Prayer:*

Father God, what can I say except, "Thank You" for giving me this wonderful gift of Salvation! Just the fact that I am saved from sin and its power and penalty, would be a huge gift in itself, especially since You offered it to me freely and while I was yet a sinner. What more could I ask for than that! Yet, for You, that was just the beginning of the abundance of your grace and mercy, for within that package of Salvation you put more Blessings than I could ever imagine! It included an unending supply of all I could ever need or want for the rest of my life! I hope I can somehow share the magnitude of this with all those I meet, so that all Believers will come to realize what they have received in Christ and Un-Believers will see what they are missing out on!

My Personal Thoughts:

Our Riches in Christ—
Spiritual Blessing—

Believers have been:

Sanctified

just as He chose us in Him before the foundation of the world, that we should be holy and without blame before Him in love, Ephesians 1:4

For we are His workmanship, created in Christ Jesus for good works, which God prepared beforehand that we should walk in them. Ephesians 2:10

Believers, we are the "set apart" ones here on earth. God chose us to reflect His glory. It is no longer about us—it is about God and His Will for our lives. He created us and He chose us, and in Christ He has made us pure and without blemish so we can be His image to this world.

We are God's workmanship, created in Christ to do the good works that He has prepared for us to do. This should make us feel special every day knowing that His work in us is ongoing and that He is continually at work in bringing us to the place where we can walk in all the good works He has planned for us to do for Him. How exciting!

WALK IT OUT—*Prayer:*

Dear Father God, You chose me in Christ to be holy, set apart, blameless, so I could come before You in love and reflect Your glory to all the world! You created me to do good works that You prepared only for me to do, so that in doing them I might be Your image here on earth! What an awesome Blessing! It makes me feel so special! Thank You, Father God, that I am once again reminded that I do have a purpose in this life and that that purpose is to serve You by doing the good works which You have prepared for me to do. I am so glad that You chose me and I pray that I will not let one day go by that I am not doing those good works that You have planned for me to do.

My Personal Thoughts:

Our Riches in Christ—
Spiritual Blessing—

Believers have been:

$\mathcal{S}eated$

who is a deposit guaranteeing our inheritance until the redemption of those who are God's possession… Ephesians1:14 (New International Version)

Believers, the Holy Spirit indwells in us as a guarantee of our inheritance. He is our security deposit on all the riches we are to receive from God. The King James Version says He is *"the earnest of our inheritance."* EARNEST is defined as "something of value given by the buyer to the seller…to bind a bargain…"[4] or as "a token of what is to come."[5] When you buy a home, you put down "earnest money," this says you are serious about fulfilling your part of the deal. The Holy Spirit is God's "earnest." His presence in us shows God is serious about fulfilling what He said He would do for us. He is God's Promise.

Jesus told His disciples to *"wait for the Promise of the Father"* (Acts 1:4). Who, He went on to explain, is the Holy Spirit.

WALK IT OUT—*Prayer:*

Dear Father God, I thank You that I am marked with Your Seal, the promised Holy Spirit. I am thankful that He dwells within me, as the guarantee of my inheritance in Christ. This knowledge should keep me from doubt and worry over my life now or what I might face in the future, because I have the assurance that I belong to You, that I am Your possession, and that You will keep me and care for me until the time of my redemption. Thank You God, that Your Promise lives within me here on earth, thus giving me the assurance that someday, I will live together with You, Him and Jesus for all eternity! Hallelujah! Amen!

---

4 en.wiktionary.org/wiki/earnest
5 en.wiktionary.org/wiki/earnest

My Personal Thoughts:

Our Riches in Christ—
Spiritual Blessing—

Believers have been:

$\mathcal{S}eated$

and [God] raised us up with Him and seated us with Him in the heavenly places in Christ Jesus… Ephesians 2:6 (English Standard Version)

Believers, the "us" is indeed us! Not only did God give us a new life in Christ, but He raised us up and Seated us with Him in the heavenlies! Christ is Seated at the right hand of the Father in the heavenly places (Eph.1:20) and so are we! Spiritually, we are in Christ and sitting right next to the Father!

Now, please take note of the word "Seated" because sitting, you know, depicts rest. Therefore, this Blessing shows us we can rest spiritually, because we are in Christ (who already did all the work) and we are Seated with Him (who is also Seated because His work is done). Christ is the Victor and in Him we find and have our victory.

Therefore, whatever happens to us physically or materially down here on earth can't affect what's going on in our inner man or in the position that we have spiritually with the Lord Jesus Christ! I want to say as Paul said in Ephesians 1:3: *"Blessed be the God and Father of our Lord Jesus Christ, who has blessed us with every spiritual blessing in the heavenly places in Christ."*

WALK IT OUT—*Prayer:*

Dear God, You have so Blessed me to be Seated in the heavenly places! Seated, resting there, even though I did no work. Seated next to You, in Christ, victorious, even though I did nothing to earn the victory. As a believer, I see I now belong to a different world, a heavenly place where I am Seated with You in Christ. Help me to remember this as I start each day because I want my earthly life to reflect the reality of my spiritual life. I want to keep my mind set on things above, where I am Seated spiritually, and not on things on this earth, so that others, believers and non-believers alike, will be able to see and know that there is something different about me because of who I am in Christ. Even though I am in this world, I am not of this world and I pray that my thoughts and actions will show that every day. Thank You, Father God for who I am and where I am in Christ! *"If then you were raised with Christ, seek those things which are above, where Christ is, sitting at the right hand of God. Set your mind on things above, not on things on the earth. For you died, and your life is hidden with Christ in God. When Christ who is our life appears, then you also will appear with Him in glory."* Colossians 3:1-4

My Personal Thoughts:

Our Riches in Christ—
Spiritual Blessing—

Believers have been given:

$\mathcal{S}$trength

that He would grant you, according to the riches of His glory, to be strengthened with might through His Spirit in the inner man...
Ephesians 3:16

God can give you so much because He has so much! He strengthens us with might proportionately from His unlimited source! Believers, that means we have a vast amount of Strength and power available to us for our inner man and we need to utilize it in order to live a victorious Christian life here on earth. Our inner man is our spirit, the spiritual part of us where the Holy Spirit dwells and works. As believers, our inner man is alive, it can see, hear, taste, and feel. It must be exercised, cleansed, and fed. (Psalms 119:18, Matthew 13:9, Psalms 34:8, Acts 17:27, 1Timothy 4:7-8, Psalms 51:7, and Matthew 4:4)

Our inner man can grow spiritually. It can be renewed and reinforced daily. Even though our outer man is declining and our physical body may not be functioning well, our inner man has unlimited power and Strength available to it daily (Psalm 73:26). Why then, do we focus so much of our attention on the physical outer man, which is weak and wasting away?

Let's not neglect our inner man, who has unlimited power, Strength and resources available through the working of the Holy Spirit within us, to enable us to live our lives as Jesus did. Let's take every opportunity we can to increase our inner man by yielding to the Holy Spirit and allowing Him to do His work in us daily. Let's work with the Holy Spirit by feeding our inner man the word of God, exercising him in obedience, cleansing him by daily prayer and utilizing his senses in praise and worship. Then, we will begin to experience the reality of this magnificent Spiritual Blessing in our lives as God's power and Strength are granted to us and we grow and become more like Christ for the glory of God!

WALK IT OUT—Prayer:

Dear Father God, what a vast resource You have made available to me! Even though my physical body may be declining, I see it is possible that my inner man can be growing stronger every day, strengthening me to face the trials and temptations here on earth, so that I can overcome them in the power of Your might! I am so blessed that You have made this possible for me and I want to start focusing on my inner man more so that he will grow and increase. Help me to remember each day to not only care for my daily physical needs but to also spend time caring for the daily spiritual needs of my inner man. May You grant me, according to the riches of Your glory, to be strengthened with might through Your Spirit in my inner man. Thank You, Father God, for the Blessings You make available to me daily.

My Personal Thoughts:

Our Riches in Christ—
Spiritual Blessing—

Believers have been given:

$$\mathcal{Success}$$

Blessed be the God and Father of our Lord Jesus Christ, who has blessed us with every spiritual blessing in the heavenly places in Christ, Ephesians 1:3

For we are His workmanship, created in Christ Jesus for good works, which God prepared beforehand that we should walk in them. Ephesians 2:10

Now to Him who is able to do exceedingly abundantly above all that we ask or think, according to the power that works in us, Ephesians 3:20

What comes to your mind when you read the above verses? A lot of things of course, but is Success one of those? Everyone wants to succeed! The world is all about success. We are taught from youth that we need to be successful. We strive to attain it. Our days are spent focusing on what we can do to "become successful" in life. As the minutes and hours of our lives pass us by, we often stop to reflect and wonder if we have achieved our goal of living a successful life. But, as Believers, our focus should be *"on things above, not on things on the earth"* (Col.3:2). As Believers, the standard of our success should be Jesus. Our goal should be to become more and more like Him every day. That is what God wants for us and we have already been given everything we need from Him to succeed spiritually so we can begin to accomplish that goal of becoming Christ-like, for from the moment we believed and received Jesus, God Blessed us with Success! We are successful because we have every Spiritual Blessing! We are successful because we are God's workmanship, His creation. We are successful because God created good works for us to do and He has blessed us with all we need to fulfill them. We are successful because we have an abundance of God's power within us, which assures us that there is no end to the Success we can realize spiritually because we have been Blessed in Christ with everything we need to succeed!

WALK IT OUT—*Prayer:*

Dear Father God, remind me to read Your word daily for that is where I will receive the truth and strength I need each day to walk in the Success You have made possible and desire for me to achieve spiritually. Help me to stay focused on things above which are eternal, and not on things here on earth which are passing away. Help me to remember to read these verses from Ephesians, and others, that show me who I really am in Christ, so on those days when I might be feeling "un-successful" and the world is telling me I am a failure, I might be reminded that I am a Success, because in Christ I cannot be a failure. Then, as I reflect Christ in my life, run the race of high calling to win the heavenly prize, and store up my treasures in heaven, I will have true Success here on earth as well as someday in heaven.

My Personal Thoughts:

_____

_____

_____

_____

_____

_____

_____

_____

_____

_____

_____

_____

_____

_____

_____

_____

_____

_____

_____

_____

Our Riches in Christ—
Spiritual Blessing—

Believers are the:

Temple of God

in whom you also are being built together for a dwelling place of God in the Spirit. Ephesians 2:22

Together, we believers are being "grown" into God's Holy Temple. Let's read what Paul says in Ephesians 2:19 thru 22: "*Now, therefore, you are no longer strangers and foreigners, but fellow citizens with the saints and members of the household of God, having been built on the foundation of the apostles and prophets, Jesus Christ Himself being the chief cornerstone, in whom the whole building, being fitted together, grows into a holy temple in the Lord, in whom you also are being built together for a dwelling place of God in the Spirit.*"

It's not just about us! It's about God and what He is accomplishing through us for His glory. As we unite with other believers we fit together and grow into a holy temple for God, a place where His Spirit can dwell on this earth, His church, and what a glorious church that is! Christ is the chief cornerstone that holds everything together, its foundation is built on the teaching of the apostles and prophets, and God's Spirit dwells there in all the fellow citizens of God. What a glorious place it must be!

Isn't it wonderful to think that we can be a part of something so great! This gives a whole new meaning to "church" doesn't it?

WALK IT OUT—*Prayer:*

Dear Father God, I am so glad to know that I am blessed to be a part of something so wonderful! It is such a Blessing to realize that Your Holy Spirit dwells within me. This is a Blessing in itself, but the realization that I am part of a much bigger plan where I am being fitted together with other believers to form a Temple for You is really amazing to me and I do so thank You for what I am becoming in Christ and the glory I am bringing to You because I am a believer!

My Personal Thoughts:

Our Riches in Christ—
Spiritual Blessing—

Believers have been given:

Understanding

He has showered His kindness on us, along with all wisdom and understanding. Ephesians 1:8 (New Living Translation)

Believers, God has lavished upon us all Understanding. Not only have we been given the Knowledge of His Will, but we also have been showered with Understanding.

What exactly is Understanding? Well, it is sometimes hard to define. It means to be able to take information and put it to practical use. It is much more than just knowledge. It is comprehension, which is the ability to know or perceive. It is the power to grasp an idea.

God has graciously given to us everything we need to live for Him. And one of the greatest gifts He has given to us is the truth of His written Word. Now, Understanding is the supernatural ability to take the truth He's given and apply it to our daily Christian walk. God not only gives us an awareness of truth, He gives us understanding in how to live it.

This is a very valuable Blessing for our day-to-day life and one we should be very thankful for because with Understanding we not only have knowledge of what is correct, we now have an awareness of how that knowledge can be used to make correct choices in our daily lives.

WALK IT OUT—*Prayer:*

Dear Father God, Thank You so much for showering Your kindness on me and for providing me the Blessing of Understanding. In my day-to-day life I need this Blessing to make correct choices. Discernment is important when I am faced with daily decisions. I often need prudence to lead me to right actions, therefore, I am so glad You have blessed me with all I need to face each day of my life here on earth.

My Personal Thoughts:

51

Our Riches in Christ— Spiritual Blessing—

Believers have been:

United With Christ

But now you belong to Christ Jesus. Though you once were far away from God, now you have been brought near to Him because of the blood of Christ. Ephesians 2:13 (New Living Translation)

"But now you belong to Christ Jesus." What is this verse really saying? Believers, it is telling us that while in the past we were separated from God by sin, aliens to hope, and strangers to His promises, we are now eternally joined to Him through the death of Jesus on the Cross. We are one with Him. We are related to Him. We have a place with Him. We are members of God's household with Him. We belong.

Everyone wants to belong to someone or something because belonging gives a special feeling of security and comfort. It makes one feel special, important, loved. We are somebody—because we belong to someone or something.

Believers, the knowledge that we now belong to Christ Jesus should make us feel so special and loved because we, who were once far away from God, are now united with Christ and with God! We are now a part of God's eternal heavenly kingdom. We belong! What a Blessing! What can we say except "Thank you, Jesus!"

WALK IT OUT—*Prayer:*

Dear God, reading this verse just makes me want ot sing and shout praises in thanksgiving to Jesus for what He did when He shed His blood for me! I want to let the world know that I belong to Jesus and to You, God, and it doesn't matter if I don't seem to fit in down here on earth, because I know I have a place waiting for me in Your heavenly kingdom where I belong. A place where I will someday dwell with You and Jesus forever! I am special. I am loved. I am important. I belong!

My Personal Thoughts:

Our Riches in Christ—
Spiritual Blessing—

Believers have been given:

Unity

And this is his plan: At the right time He [God] will bring everything together under the authority of Christ—everything in heaven and on earth. Ephesians 1:10 (New Living Translation)

God had a plan from the beginning: He purposed that all creation (man, animals, earth, cosmos) would one day be in Unity. All *the creation looks forward to the day when it will join God's children in glorious freedom from death and decay,* (Romans 8:21 New Living Translation).

In God's time, that plan will come to fruition and all things will come together in heaven and earth. God's redemptive plan will be put into effect and there will be complete Unity of all creation. The original harmony of the universe will be restored and all will be one under Christ.

...that at the name of Jesus every knee should bow, of those in heaven, and of those on earth, and of those under the earth, Philippians 2:10

WALK IT OUT—*Prayer:*

Dear Father God, I am so glad to know that I will be a part of this wonderful Unity in heaven and earth! I am eagerly awaiting the coming together of all things, and can only imagine the wonder of living in a restored universe where all will be one under Christ! However, as I wait and anticipate this happening, I know there is work yet to do, for so many do not know You or Your Son and they have no idea of Your wonderful plan of restoration and Unity. So I will pray for those who haven't yet believed and received, that they may also come to know Christ and be a part of this Unity. I also pray that You, Father God, will work through me in whatever way You may choose, to draw those who need salvation to You Father, so they might come to know Jesus and be saved.

My Personal Thoughts:

Our Riches in Christ——
Spiritual Blessing——

Believers have been given:

Wisdom

that the God of our Lord Jesus Christ, the Father of glory, may give to you the spirit of wisdom and revelation in the knowledge of Him, Ephesians 1:17

to the intent that now the manifold wisdom of God might be made known by the church to the principalities and powers in the heavenly places, Ephesians 3:10

Believers, we are blessed with the Wisdom of God! The Holy Spirit dwells within us and leads us to all truth. He "quickens" us with Wisdom and revelation. Why? So that we might have knowledge of God and make that knowledge known to the principalities and powers in the heavenly places! We are the church. We are to shine as many faceted gems, giving off the Wisdom of God and reflecting His glory.

"The wisdom of God displayed in creation and embodied in Christ is a many splendored thing, iridescent with constantly unfolding beauties." (The Expositor's Bible Commentary, Volume 11. Copyright ©1981 by Zondervan)

WALK IT OUT—*Prayer:*

Dear God, thank you for this wonderful blessing of Your Wisdom. I pray that Your Holy Spirit might quicken me to use it daily so that You might be made known to the principalities and powers in heavenly places. What an awesome thought that is! That You could be made known by me! I pray that I can remind myself of this each day and so shine forth Your manifold Wisdom for all to see!

My Personal Thoughts:

Our Riches in Christ—
Spiritual Blessing—

Believers are the:

Workmanship of God

For we are His workmanship, created in Christ Jesus for good works, which God prepared beforehand that we should walk in them. Ephesians 2:10

For we are God's masterpiece. He has created us anew in Christ Jesus, so that we can do the good things he planned for us long ago. Ephesians 2:10 (New Living Translation)

The Greek word for Workmanship is poiēma which means poem. So that would mean, believers, that we are God's poem, and according to the Dictionary our definition is:

1. A verbal composition designed to convey experiences, ideas, or emotions in a vivid and imaginative way, characterized by the use of language chosen for its sound and suggestive power and by the use of literary techniques such as meter, metaphor, and rhyme. 2. A composition in verse rather than in prose. 3. A literary composition written with an intensity or beauty of language more characteristic of poetry than of prose. 4. A creation, object, or experience having beauty suggestive of poetry.[6]

We are POETRY—NOT PROSE…What is PROSE?

1. Ordinary speech or writing, without metrical structure. 2. Commonplace expression or quality.[7]

We are GOD'S MASTERPIECE, which is:

1. An outstanding work, achievement, or performance 2. The most outstanding piece of work of a creative artist, craftsman, etc.[8]

Pretty impressive isn't it! Believers, we are blessed to be God's "verbal composition" meaning we are put together by God's speech, which is not just ordinary speech, but it is a language full of sound and power which creates something beautiful! We are a Poetic Masterpiece! Why did God bless us to be "His Poem"? In order that we might make Him known to the world. We are an extension of Him, a reflection of His image. We are His words put together to bring His beautiful message of love to those around us. We are an expression of His ideas. We are a "rhythmical creation of beauty" (Edgar Allen Poe's definition of poetry) and our author is God!

---

6 The American Heritage Dictionary, Fourth Edition, 2000
7 The American Heritage Dictionary, Fourth Edition, 2000
8 Collins English Dictionary – Complete and Unabridged, 2003

WALK IT OUT—*Prayer:*

My heart is overflowing with a good theme; I recite my composition concerning the King; My tongue is the pen of a ready writer (Psalm 45:1).

Dear God, what can I, Your Poem, say to You? What can a creation say to its Creator? It can speak Your words back to You in praise and thanksgiving. It can bring You joy as You look upon it and see it doing just what You created it to do. It can carry the beauty You put into it wherever it goes and so bless You as it blesses others. It can convey You to the world. Yes, dear God, and that is exactly what I hope to do. I want to be known as "Your Love Sonnet" to the world. I want others to "read" me each day and come to know You as I do. Thank You for creating me and blessing me. May I bring You glory each day in all I say and do.

My Personal Thoughts:

Acknowledgments

I want to thank my friend, Rev. Richard L. Rice, for always being willing to help me with my many questions on the Spiritual Blessings. His answers were a valuable addition to this book and I would not have been able to put it all together without his knowledge, insight and help. His friendship has been such a blessing in my life.

I want to thank my friend, Sherry Green, for volunteering her time to edit and design this book. Sherry has been a true blessing in my life and I so appreciate all the time she has freely given to help me get this book published.

I want to thank my friends and fellow believers who have encouraged me and prayed for me while I was working on putting all of this together.

I also want to acknowledge the many people in the Spiritual Blessings Groups who sent me encouraging messages and thanks at the times when copies of these individual Spiritual Blessings were being sent out to them via email through my online ministry *Smile God Loves You* at www.smilegodlovesyou.org

Each thank you and encouraging message showed me that there was a need for this book to be published and those messages, at times, were just the thing that kept me focused on doing what was needed to get this book published.

Authors Bio

It is my greatest desire to know the hope of His calling and to walk in it daily

—Ephesians 1:18 and 4:1

Leona J. Atkinson is an inspirational freelance writer who lives in Portland, Oregon. She has had an online encouragement ministry called Smile God Loves You since 1997 (www.smilegodlovesyou.org). Visit her personal website at www.leonaatkinson.com or visit her blog at http://spiritualblessingsblog.wordpress.com

Rev. Richard L. Rice lives outside of Portland, Oregon. He is a local pastor, in the Christian ministry since 1986. Visit his persoanal blog, "Where Living Begins" (Random Thoughts from the Bible and Life) at http://calvaryopenbible.wordpress.com/

Made in the USA
Monee, IL
17 September 2020